HIGH SCHOOL MUSICAL

TRIVIA & QUIZ BOOK

EXPERT EDITION

By Emma Harrison

Based on "High School Musical", written by Peter Barsocchini
Based on "High School Musical 2," Written by Peter Barsocchini
Based on Characters Created by Peter Barsocchini

New York

Printed in the United States of America

First Edition
1 3 5 7 9 10 8 6 4 2

Library of Congress Control Number: 2007930136
ISBN-13: 978-1-4231-0828-3
ISBN-10: 1-4231-0828-0

For more Disney Press fun, visit www.disneybooks.com
Visit DisneyChannel.com

Every true-blue *High School Musical* fan knows that Troy is captain of the varsity basketball team, that Gabriella once won a science trophy, and that Sharpay and Ryan are co–presidents of the drama club. But can you name East High's biggest rival school or the two lead characters in *Twinkle Towne*? Better get'cha head in the game, because we're about to test your *High School Musical* knowledge big-time!

WILDCAT QUIZ #1

1. What is Troy's last name?
   A. Baylor
   B. Baxter
   C. Bolton

2. What technology does Ms. Darbus consider a menace?
   A. DVD players
   B. Alarm clocks
   C. Cell phones

3. When Gabriella's mom tells her to go to the New Year's Eve party, what is Gabriella doing?
   A. Chatting with friends
   B. Reading a book
   C. Watching the fire in the fireplace

4. Why do Gabriella and her mom move to Albuquerque?
   A. Mrs. Montez's company moves her there.
   B. Gabriella didn't like her old school.
   C. Gabriella wanted to go to school with Troy.

5. On her first day at East High, what is Gabriella afraid of becoming?

    A. The head cheerleader
    B. The school's freaky genius girl
    C. The school drama queen

6. Ryan and Sharpay are:

    A. Cousins
    B. Brother and sister
    C. Archenemies

7. How does Taylor find out that Gabriella is so smart?

    A. Gabriella tells her.
    B. Sharpay puts an article about Gabriella in Taylor's locker.
    C. Taylor quizzes Gabriella.

8. Which of these guys is on the Wildcats basketball team?

    A. Troy
    B. Ryan
    C. Zeke
    D. A and C
    E. All of the above

3

ANSWERS:

1. C   5. B
2. C   6. B
3. B   7. B
4. A   8. D

SCORING:

Give yourself two points
for each correct answer.

If you scored:

0-4
Get'cha head in the game!

Maybe another viewing of
High School Musical will get
your Wildcat pride pumping!

6-10
You've got some Wildcat spirit.

You know the basics, but you
might want to hit the books
before taking Wildcat Quiz #2!

12-16
You're a true Wildcat!

You clearly know a lot about
East High and its students.
Now check out Wildcat Quiz
#2 on page 18 to see if you can
keep the pride alive!

WERE YOU BORN FOR STARDOM?

Ever since she was a little girl, Sharpay Evans has been starring in musicals and plays. She *loves* to be the center of attention, and not only is she supertalented, but she works hard to make sure that every audition piece is just right. Think you've got what it takes to be a star like Sharpay? Take this quiz and find out!

1. **On the morning announcements, you hear that the sign-up sheet for musical auditions has been posted in the hall. You:**
   A. Consider signing up, but wait until the end of the day so you can see who the competition will be.
   B. Run out the door before the bell even rings and sign your name to the sheet in huge letters.
   C. Feel nervous at the very thought and avoid the hallway with the sign-up sheet in it all day.

2. **The lead actress in the school play gets laryngitis the week before the production. The director asks you to take her place. The show must go on, after all! You:**
   A. Start memorizing the script right away and get the crew to put your name on the star's dressing room.
   B. Run right to the star's house and administer hot tea with lemon. You'll cure her if it kills you.
   C. Say you'll do it if he wants, but secretly hope the star gets better.

3. You're standing in the wings during the musical and the soloist onstage forgets the words to the song she's singing. You:

    A. Whisper the words from the wings until she remembers them.

    B. Run out onstage and sing the song for her.

    C. Hide backstage until it's over. You can't even watch.

4. As you wait backstage before your first audition, you are:

    A. Confidently practicing your steps and going over your song.

    B. Huddled near the wall, crying, and wondering why you're doing this.

    C. Cheering others on while patiently waiting your turn.

5. Imagine yourself walking down a red carpet to your first movie premiere, flanked by reporters and photographers. You are:

    A. Striding along with a group of your friends, smiling and laughing.

    B. Strutting solo, striking poses for the photographers. You've known which side was your best since kindergarten.

    C. Speed-walking with your head down.

6. You hear that the pretty new girl in school is going to be trying out for the part that you want in the musical. You:

    A. Don't bother auditioning—you know she'll get the part.

    B. Wish her luck and then do your best.

    C. Ignore her so she'll think everyone in drama club is mean and she won't try out at all.

1. A-1   B-2   C-0
2. A-2   B-0   C-1
3. A-1   B-2   C-0
4. A-2   B-0   C-1
5. A-1   B-2   C-0
6. A-0   B-1   C-2

If you scored:

0-4

Backstage Baby!

If the very idea of being in the spotlight gives you the shivers, you might want to consider taking a backstage role. The people behind the scenes are just as important as the stars!

5-8

There's No "I" in Theater

You've got the confidence and the attitude to be a star. But seeing your name in lights is not as important to you as putting on a successful show with the rest of the cast—no matter how big or small your role is. Now that's the kind of player we want on our stage.

9-12

Born to Be a Star!

You live for the spotlight and know just how to get what you need in order to succeed. But you'd better take a second look at the way you treat other people. You don't want to hurt anyone on your way to the top!

7

WHICH HIGH SCHOOL MUSICAL GIRL ARE YOU?

Are you the sweet, shy type like Gabriella? Do you slay your friends with your wit and brains like Taylor? Or do you rule the school like drama queen Sharpay? Think you know which *High School Musical* character you're most like? The answer might surprise you. (After all, Gabriella never thought she was star material and look what she ended up accomplishing!) Take this quiz and find out which role you fit into! (And remember, answer honestly.)

1. **At a party, a girl you don't know comes over and starts talking to you. You:**
    A. Tell her you can't talk right now. You're too busy fixing your hair.
    B. Ask her a few brainteasers to see if she's worth talking to.
    C. Smile politely, blush, and wonder why she chose to talk to you.

2. **When you walk down the hallway at school. You:**
    A. Walk right down the center and expect everyone to get out of your way.
    B. Walk with your friends, going over the homework for next period.
    C. Walk along with a friendly smile for everyone you pass.

3. **Finish this sentence: "Making new friends is _____"**
    A. "Exciting! Most people love me."
    B. "Fine. But I usually have something more important to do."
    C. "Scary. I never know what to say."

4. **You see someone acting like a jerk or doing something you don't like. You:**
    A. Tell him to quit it. It's irritating you.
    B. Roll your eyes and ignore him until he goes away.
    C. Figure he must be having a bad day and see if you can help.

5. **You drop your tray in the middle of the cafeteria and everyone laughs. You:**
    A. Tell them off. How dare they laugh at you?
    B. Immediately start calculating whether you have enough money left to buy another lunch.
    C. Blush, then laugh with them. After all, everyone has embarrassing moments, but it helps to have a sense of humor about them!

6. You get called on in class when you aren't paying attention. You:

    A. Rant to the teacher about how unfair his stealth questions are.

    B. Ask him to repeat the question and then quickly figure out the answer.

    C. Are so embarrassed you can barely speak or think.

7. One of your friends wants to take up snowboarding but has never expressed an interest in it before. You:

    A. Freak out and tell her if she does this, you'll never talk to her again. You hate change.

    B. Try to talk her out of it. It's *so* not her.

    C. Tell her you think it's great that she wants to try new things.

SCORING:

MOSTLY A'S:
You are SHARPAY!
A diva all the way, you know you're a star and you act like it. Everyone else better get out of your way!

MOSTLY B'S:
You are TAYLOR!
You are a serious student and a serious person, but you know how to have fun when the time is right.

MOSTLY C'S:
You are GABRIELLA!
You can be shy, but you're also a genuinely nice person who wants everyone around you to be happy.

TAKE A CHANCE

Everyone at East High was shocked when Gabriella and Troy auditioned for the school musical, *Twinkle Towne*. They each took a big chance going out there to try something new, and the results were incredible! Are you willing to try new things, or do you let opportunities pass you by? Take this quiz and find out!

1. **The new girl at school is starting a lacrosse team. You've never played before but think it looks like fun. When you see her in the cafeteria you:**
   A. Walk right over and tell her you're in.
   B. Wander over and ask her a zillion questions about the sport, then tell her you have to think about it.
   C. Ignore the urge. You'd probably stink at it anyway!

2. **The boss at your part-time job wants to promote you from ice-cream scooper to cashier. You:**
   A. Say, "No thanks." You're good at scooping, and you'd like to stick with it.
   B. Get so stressed out about learning something new and potentially messing it up, you have to quit.
   C. Say, "Sounds good! When do I start training?"

3. **You joined the choir because you needed an elective, but you've started to really like singing. Your director asks if you'd like to try a solo at the next concert. You:**
   A. Say, "Yes!" You're SO excited.
   B. Freak out and say, "No." You'd rather die.
   C. Feel a bit unsure but agree to give it a try.

4. You have a crush on the cute new guy in school. You:

    A. Giggle every time he walks into a room but never talk to him.

    B. Get a friend to ask him if he likes you.

    C. Walk right over to him and ask him if he wants to hang out.

5. You buy a funky dress you really like, but your best friend says it's too weird. You:

    A. Wear it anyway. You like it.

    B. Put it in the back of your closet and forget it exists.

    C. Wear it, but only to places where you know no one from school will ever see you.

6. You've decided to cut your hair really short. When the stylist asks if you're sure, you:

    A. Say, "No. Just trim it." (You can always go short next time.)

    B. Brace yourself and say, "Yes. Do it!"

    C. Split the difference and have a couple inches taken off.

7. Your teacher is in the middle of a history lesson when he gets a date wrong. You:

    A. Raise your hand and correct him.

    B. Wait until after class and tell him you think he misspoke.

    C. Do nothing—except make sure *you've* got it right in your notes.

SCORING:

Did You Know?

The next time you watch *High School Musical*, look for how often the color red appears in the movie. The director used red a lot because he thought the color had power and energy.

If you scored:

0–4
Play-It-Safer

You're afraid of getting rejected, embarrassed, and teased. But if you don't try new things, your life will be pretty boring. You may be surprised at what happens when you try something new.

5–9
Kinda Daring

You know how to lead a balanced life. Sometimes you try a new activity; other times you like to stick with what already works. Sounds like you really know who you are and what you want!

10–14
Risk-Taker

If there's a limb out there, you're on it! You're beyond brave, and we admire your ability to get out there and try new things. But please draw the line at fire-eating and BASE jumping.

HOW MOLDABLE ARE YOU?

Sometimes it's easy to be true to yourself. Like when you're picking out your breakfast cereal or deciding which TV show to watch. But other times, it seems as if everyone has an opinion on everything you do. Your friends, your parents, even your teachers try to tell you what classes to take, what activities to participate in, what kind of person you should be. It can get exhausting. (Just ask Troy and Gabriella!) Are you skilled at staying true to yourself, or do you let the people around you mold you? Take this quiz, and you'll see just how claylike (or not) you really are!

I. **It's time to pick classes for next year. You really want to take creative writing, but all your friends are talking about how incredible fashion design is going to be. You:**

    A. Stick to creative writing. You want to be a writer someday, not a fashion designer.

    B. Sign up for fashion design. All your friends are going to be in the class, and you'll miss out on so much hang time if you don't take it.

    C. Try to figure out how you can do both.

2. **You and the girls are deciding on a movie to rent this Friday night. They want a romantic comedy, but you really want to see the new fantasy flick. Plus, they got to pick last time. You:**
   A. Insist that it's your turn to pick the movie and make them all watch your fantasy film.
   B. Compromise. Rent both and see if you can stay up long enough to watch them.
   C. Don't even mention the fantasy flick. You know they'd think it's uncool.

3. **You want to join the new environmental club at school, but it conflicts with the French club, which you're sort of over anyway. Problem is, your mom thinks French club is important for your college applications. You:**
   A. Don't even bother talking to your mom about it. It's pointless. You'll stay in French club.
   B. Write down your list of reasons for switching and then present them to your mom. How could she say no to such a reasonable approach?
   C. Make the switch in secret. It's your life, and she won't know until it's too late anyway.

4. **Your friends decide that Thursday is going to be pink day from now on—you're all going to wear pink. They're all excited about the plan. You, unfortunately, happen to hate pink. You:**
   A. Tell them you won't be wearing pink, and anyone who tries to make you conform like that is not your friend.
   B. Wear pink on Thursday.
   C. Show up on Thursday in black and hope for the best, but bring a pink headband in case of a total meltdown.

5. **You're on the dance committee, and everyone has already decided that "City Lights" is going to be the theme. You think "City Lights" is lame and overused. One of the girls in charge asks what you think of the theme. You:**
   - A: Tell her you think it's a fabulous idea.
   - B: Tell her it's okay, but ask if you can't keep brainstorming and see if you can come up with something more fresh.
   - C: Tell them if they insist on using that theme that you're going to quit the committee.

6. **You wear your favorite jeans to school, and the most popular girl in your class picks on them, saying they're so last year. You:**
   - A. Tell her off. Who is she to comment on your clothes?
   - B. Feel miserable for the rest of the day and throw the jeans out when you get home.
   - C. Ignore her and walk away, but wonder if maybe you shouldn't save up for some new clothes.

SCORING:

1. A-2 B-0 C-1
2. A-2 B-1 C-0
3. A-0 B-1 C-2
4. A-2 B-0 C-1
5. A-0 B-1 C-2
6. A-2 B-0 C-1

If you scored:

0-4

Clay All the Way

It's time for you to start sticking up for yourself! If you keep letting other people run your life, then your life isn't your own. Figure out what you like, and if somebody challenges you, stick to your guns. Not only will it feel good, but it may open their eyes to a different way of thinking.

5-8

Somewhat Moldable

You know what you want and who you are, but sometimes you fall victim to peer pressure. Just make sure you keep standing up for yourself when it's really important.

9-12

True-Blue You!

Wow! You really know who you are, and you let everyone know it! We applaud your self-confidence, but you should be careful not to impose your beliefs on other people. They're entitled to their opinions just as you're entitled to yours. Oh, and if you answered "C" to number three, you may want to talk to your parents and let them in on your after-school activities.

WILDCAT QUIZ #2

So you did okay on the first Wildcat Quiz, and you're feeling good. Well, buckle up, Wildcat, because the questions are about to get harder! Check out these puzzlers based on *High School Musical* and find out if you know as much as you think you do.

1. **We all know that *High School Musical* takes place at East High. But what's the name of the Wildcats' rival school?**
   A. Southeast High
   B. West High
   C. North High

2. **In which of the fifty states is East High located?**
   A. Colorado
   B. Arizona
   C. New Mexico

3. **Before Gabriella arrives, how many times has Taylor's Scholastic Decathlon team won the championship?**
   A. Once
   B. Twice
   C. Never

4. In the cafeteria scene, the skater dude confesses he plays what instrument?
   A. The cello
   B. The violin
   C. The flute

5. Which of these characters was on the East High basketball team as a kid?
   A. Coach Bolton
   B. Principal Matsui
   C. Ms. Darbus

6. What team does Gabriella eventually join at East High?
   A. The debate team
   B. The Scholastic Decathlon team
   C. The cheerleading squad

7. What's the first song Gabriella and Troy sing together in *High School Musical*?
   A. "What I've Been Looking For"
   B. "Breaking Free"
   C. "Start of Something New"

8. Who is the captain of the Wildcats basketball team?
   A. Chad
   B. Troy
   C. Zeke

ANSWERS:

1. B
2. C
3. C
4. A
5. A
6. B
7. C
8. B

SCORING:

Give yourself two points for each correct answer.

If you scored:

0–4
You need a refresher course!

Did you say you'd seen this movie? Seems more like you dozed through it.

6–10
Taylor McKessie might hang out with you.

You know your stuff, but maybe not quite enough to be in with the smartest kids at East High.

12–16
Nice to meet you, freaky genius girl!

You may just be as smart as Gabriella. Well, at least when it comes to *High School Musical* trivia!

HOW ACCEPTING ARE YOU?

Both Taylor and Chad kind of flipped out when they discovered their friends Gabriella and Troy were auditioning for the musical. Gabriella was supposed to be all about her classes, and Troy was supposed to be all about basketball. Taylor and Chad were scared that their friends were changing . . . so they tried to change them back. And we all know how that worked out—not well! Are you able to accept your friends for who they are, even if they don't stick to the status quo? Take this quiz and find out!

1. You and your best friend have been taking ballet lessons together since nursery school, but this year she's decided to try out for the soccer team instead. You:
- A. Wish her luck.
- B. Tell her you can't wait to see her first game.
- C. Try to talk her out of leaving ballet class, and if that doesn't work, shut her out. Clearly she doesn't want to hang with you anymore.

2. One of your friends shows up at school with her hair dyed purple. You:
- A. Decide you have nothing in common and stop talking to her.
- B. Say it looks great, even though you think it's a hair "don't."
- C. Congratulate her on her bravery (and when she wants to dye it back, offer your help).

3. **You walk into your best friend's bedroom and her stereo is blasting some crazy type of music you think sounds awful. You:**
   A: Try to get into it. If she likes it, it must be cool.
   B. Ask her if you can change it, then pop in a CD you both love.
   C. Ask if she's totally lost her hearing, or her mind, or both.

4. **You and your BFF have always talked about attending the same college—then one day she announces that she's going to work for a year after high school instead. You:**
   A. Tell her she'll fall behind everyone else and ruin her career plans if she delays college.
   B. Agree that a little break can be a good thing, but make her promise she'll visit you at college.
   C. Say, "Whatever. Maybe college isn't for you after all."

5. **Your friend has started hanging out with another clique at school. One day she tells you she's going to cut class and go to the mall with them. You:**
   A. Say, "I'm not sure that's a good idea" and try to talk her out of it.
   B. Report her to the principal immediately.
   C. Shrug and say, "Whatever."

6. **Your best friend decides to go bungee jumping to impress a boy she's crushing on (without telling her parents, of course!). You:**
   A. Say, "Good luck!" and let her go.
   B. Ask her why she wants to do something dangerous and try to talk her out of it.
   C. Tell her she's totally lost her mind and refuse to talk to her anymore.

If you scored:

0-4
A Little Too Laid Back

You let your friends do their own thing, which is great—but you may take "live and let live" too far. If you feel left out when your friend tries something new, you should be honest with her. And if she's doing something that worries you, you should definitely speak up!

5-8
Just Right

You're supportive of your friends . . . as long as they don't get totally out of control. Kudos on knowing when to butt in and when to keep your nose out of their business.

9-12
So Judgmental!

You have a lot of opinions, and everyone knows it. But you may be too judgmental, and you could lose friends that way. Remember, one day *you* may want to make a change, and you'll want to have some friends around to support you.

WHAT'S YOUR HIGH SCHOOL MUSICAL THEME SONG?

Every music lover needs a theme song. Take this quiz to find out which of these *High School Musical* songs was written just for you!

1. You find out the school dance you've been looking forward to all year has been canceled. You:

    A. Get all your friends together to form a protest or petition the school board.

    B. Request a one-on-one meeting with the principal and give an impassioned speech about why the dance is so important to you.

    C. Let it go. You're sure they had a good reason.

2. You and your friends are all going to hang out this Saturday night. To make it a fun night, you:

    A. Come up with a cool new activity for everyone to try.

    B. Figure out a way you can be the center of attention.

    C. Suggest that everyone go out for pizza—after all, that's what you do every Friday night.

3. After school, you're most likely to be found:

    A. At a club meeting or a team practice. You belong to a lot of different organizations.

    B. Practicing your autograph or rehearsing a solo for the upcoming choral show.

    C. Playing video games with the same group of friends you always hang with.

4. You find out that you and your best friend are both up for the lead in the school play. You've starred in several plays, but she's never been interested before. You:

    A. Help each other rehearse. May the best actress win!

    B. Work harder than ever on your audition piece and tell the director that your best friend doesn't really seem to want the role at all.

    C. Tell your BFF you don't understand why she's trying out when she never has before.

5. You're assigned to a group project with three people you've never spoken to before. The group has a hard time getting organized and figuring out who should do what. You:

    A. Suggest you put all the jobs in a hat and pick at random. It's the only fair way to solve the problem and keep you all involved.

    B. Take charge and assign everyone a job, reserving the most important task for yourself. Some people were born to lead—like you!

    C. Ask the teacher if you can switch to another group—one with people you already know.

6. If your life were a play and you could rewrite it any way you liked, you would:

    A. Put in parts for all your friends.

    B. Write a starring role for yourself.

    C. Not change a word!

SCORING:

MOSTLY A'S
Your theme song is "We're All in This Together"
You are all about teamwork and hanging out with your friends. You accept people for who they are and know that everyone is a star in his or her own way.

MOSTLY B'S
Your theme song is "Bop to the Top"
You do your best to stand out from the crowd. You know you were born to be a star and you'll do everything you can to achieve your goals.

MOSTLY C'S
Your theme song is "Stick to the Status Quo"
You like your life just the way it is. Anybody who ever tries to change it on you better watch his or her back!

WHICH HIGH SCHOOL MUSICAL GUY IS RIGHT FOR YOU?

The halls of East High are just full of crush-worthy guys, and they're all very different. So which one is right for you—Troy, Chad, or Ryan? Take this quiz to find out where your Wildcat heart lies.

1. **Personal style can tell you a lot about a guy. Your man rolls into school each day wearing:**
    A. Three watches on one arm and a T-shirt with a crazy saying on it. Style *is* all about attitude.
    B. School colors. My guy is all about school spirit.
    C. Who knows, but he'll definitely be sporting a hat.

2. Your idea of a perfect Valentine's Day gift from a crush is:

A. A joke book, a CD featuring your favorite stand-up comic, or a funny DVD—anything that makes you laugh.

B. Something sweet and thoughtful, like a homemade card.

C. A song, written and performed just for you—with an accompanying dance number.

3. You walk into the cafeteria at lunchtime and spot your guy. What's he doing?

A. Telling jokes and cracking everyone up.

B. Chatting with people from all different cliques. He's popular with everyone and knows the name of every kid who strolls by.

C. Listening to his MP3 player and singing to himself, or trying out some new dance moves.

4. **Which of these comes closest to your idea of a dream date?**
   A. Something offbeat, such as a date to play miniature golf—blindfolded.
   B. A private picnic in the park.
   C. Taking in a Broadway show.

5. **Your guy got a part-time job this summer to save up for:**
   A. A car. He lives in the now. And in the now, he wants some sweet wheels.
   B. College. He's responsible and knows he has to plan for the future.
   C. Work? He doesn't need to work. His family is made of money, so he has tons of leisure time.

Did You Know?

The basketballs used during filming were smaller than regular basketballs. That helped the actors control the balls more easily during all those fast-paced action scenes. Bart Johnson (Coach Bolton) and the team practiced basketball drills for two weeks before filming started—and Bart and Zac Efron (Troy) shot baskets together almost every day they were filming.

6. **Your crush asks you to catch a movie this weekend. You get together to choose a flick and decide on:**
    - A. Any movie described in reviews as laugh-out-loud funny.
    - B. A romantic comedy, naturally. What better to get your guy in the mood to put his arm around you?
    - C. A larger-than-life musical. They put stars in your eyes and a song in your heart—and your crush feels the same way.

7. **When a guy picks you up for a date, he always brings along:**
    - A. A good joke.
    - B. Flowers.
    - C. A mix CD.

SCORING:

MOSTLY A'S:

Your *High School Musical* crush is CHAD!

You like a funny guy who's all about having a good time. Together you two will not only have a lot of laughs, but you'll rule the school.

MOSTLY B'S:

Your *High School Musical* crush is TROY!

Sweet, sensitive, and undeniably cool, your perfect guy is thoughtful and kind and not afraid to be himself. You can bet that no matter what, he'll always be there for you.

MOSTLY C'S:

Your *High School Musical* crush is RYAN!

Your dream guy is a true individual with his own dreams and goals—namely seeing his name in lights. And you have no problem being right there with him to cheer him on.

WILDCAT QUIZ #3

Okay. So you've passed the first two Wildcat Quizzes with flying colors, but are you really ready to show your Wildcat pride? This is the last set of questions from *High School Musical,* which means they're also the toughest. Put your thinking caps on (or maybe try on one of Ryan's funky hats instead). . . . Now get to it!

1. **What are the names of the lead characters in *Twinkle Towne*?**
    A. Minnie and Arnold
    B. Minnie and Mickey
    C. Kelsi and Jason

2. **What word does Sharpay think is not in Troy's vocabulary?**
    A. "Lose"
    B. "Impossible"
    C. "Fun"

3. **Which of these classrooms does Troy cut through to get to the winter-musical auditions?**
    A. The home-economics kitchen
    B. The woodworking shop
    C. The auto shop

4. **When Taylor is trying to convince Gabriella to forget auditions and concentrate on the Scholastic Decathlon, what does she call Troy?**
    A. A dumb jock
    B. Lunkhead basketball man
    C. Superstar

5. Chad claims he's been behind on homework since when?

    A. The beginning of the year

    B. The beginning of high school

    C. Preschool

6. In homeroom, which character asks Ms. Darbus how her holidays were?

    A. Zeke

    B. Sharpay

    C. Jason

7. Before *Twinkle Towne*, Kelsi's compositions were chosen for how many musicals?

    A. None

    B. One

    C. Three

8. What is Gabriella wearing when she first takes the stage at callbacks?

    A. A red dress

    B. A lab coat

    C. Jeans and a shirt

ANSWERS:

1. A   5. C
2. B   6. C
3. C   7. A
4. B   8. B

SCORING:

Give yourself two points for each correct answer.

If you scored:

0–4
Start of Something New

As in, you should start over and watch the movie one more time before taking these quizzes again.

6–10
Bop to the Top

You're climbing that ladder of success! With a little more work, you may just reach the top.

12–16
Breaking Free

Congratulations! You're soaring above the rest!

ARE YOU A SCHEMER?

When Taylor and Chad found out that Troy and Gabriella were trying out for the winter musical, they knew they had to stop them. Not only did they trick Troy into saying some things that hurt Gabriella's feelings, but they made sure Gabriella would hear and see the whole thing. And it worked! For a few days, anyway. How far would you go to get what you wanted? Take this quiz to find out.

1. **You overhear your mother telling your brother that you're having tuna casserole for dinner. You hate tuna casserole. You:**
   A. Ask her to please, please, *please* make something else.
   B. Tell her she's worked hard enough today, and you want to make dinner. Then make your favorite: mac and cheese, and hot dogs.
   C. Steal all the tuna out of the fridge and hide it under your bed.

2. **It's dodgeball day in gym—the most humiliating day of the year. You:**
   A. Suck it up and play. Everyone has to.
   B. Fake a leg cramp, fall on the floor crying, and get sent to the nurse.
   C. Get your classmates to form a formal protest. Even if it doesn't technically work, at least it'll shorten your time on the court.

3. **True or False: I have secretly read my friends' e-mails.**
   True
   False

4. Your friend Jenny is grounded and won't be allowed to come to your birthday party. You:

    A. Call her parents and say that if Jenny doesn't come to your birthday it will affect your ability to make friends for the rest of your life.

    B. Wish that she could be there, but know there's nothing you can do.

    C. Tell everyone that the party has been relocated to Jenny's house. Once half the school descends on their place with presents and cake, her parents won't be able to do anything about it.

5. Your friend wants to quit the volleyball team right before the big game. You know she's quitting because she's afraid she'll be outplayed by her rival on the other team. You:

    A. Try to talk her out of leaving. The team needs her!

    B. Get the coach to guilt her out of it.

    C. Convince her rival to call your friend a chicken. That'll get her riled up and ready to play!

6. You're dying to get a bike this Christmas, but your parents think you'll never ride it, so it won't be worth the money. You:

    A. Apply for a job delivering newspapers and show them how much money you'll earn in the first three months, making the bike totally worth it. (Of course, you don't actually intend to take the job.)

    B. Start leaving pictures of the bike all over the house until they can't take it anymore, and they cave.

    C. Let it go and hope they take pity on you and change their minds.

7. True or False: I have secretly listened in on other people's calls.

    True

    False

8. True or False: I have tried to guess someone else's computer password.

    True

    False

SCORING:

1. A-0 B-1 C-2
2. A-0 B-2 C-1
3. True: 2 False: 0
4. A-1 B-0 C-2
5. A-0 B-1 C-2
6. A-2 B-1 C-0
7. True: 2 False: 0
8. True: 2 False: 0

If you scored:

0-5
Straight Shooter

You take the honest approach ninety-nine percent of the time. You are levelheaded and trustworthy.

6-11
Only When Necessary

You're an honest person for the most part, but every once in a while, you pull off a little scheme.

12-16
A Scheme a Day

Can we trust anything you say or do? If you pull too many fast ones on your friends, they won't be around for long.

WHAT'S YOUR HIGH SCHOOL MUSICAL STYLE?

If you saw a picture of Gabriella, Sharpay, and Taylor standing next to each other, but couldn't see their faces and hairstyles, you'd still be able to tell who was who right away. Why? Because each of the girls has her own individual style. Gabriella is sweet and girly. Sharpay is trendy all the way, and Taylor is no-nonsense preppy. Which of these styles is most like your own? Take our high-fashion quiz and find out!

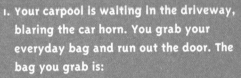

1. **Your carpool is waiting in the driveway, blaring the car horn. You grab your everyday bag and run out the door. The bag you grab is:**
   A. A basic messenger bag with some personal touches, such as pins and ribbons.
   B. Everyday bag? Who has one bag to use every day? You've got ten, at least.
   C. A practical backpack or rolling bag to hold all your books.

2. **When it comes to accessories, your philosophy is:**
   A. Small, simple, classic.
   B. As big and sparkly as possible, please!
   C. A headband now and then is cool. Maybe a necklace. That's about it.

3. **A makeover show has chosen you as its next subject. The kooky host barrels into your room and whips open your closet. What does she find inside?**

    A. Cute sweaters, girly blouses, and skirts in various pastel colors

    B. Hundreds of trendy pieces ripped right from the pages of the latest magazines

    C. Sensible blazers, knee-length skirts, and comfortable shoes

4. **There's a big party this weekend, and everyone's freaking out about what to wear. You:**

    A. Choose something pretty from your closet—something just slightly dressier than what you wear every day to school.

    B. Head straight to the mall with Daddy's credit card for a shopping spree. There's nothing worthy in your closet.

    C. Wear the same stuff you usually wear. You're no fashion victim.

5. **Finish this sentence: "When it comes to patterns, I usually choose ____."**

    A. Floral.

    B. Sequins.

    C. Solids.

6. Where can you be found on an average summer day (and what would you be wearing)?

   A. Sitting with a good book in the park, wearing a pretty sundress.
   B. Strutting your bikini by the pool.
   C. Volunteering or working at a part-time job in shorts and a polo.

7. Finish this sentence: "I most often wear my hair _____"

   A. In a soft, flirty style.
   B. Big and glamorous.
   C. In a low-maintenance style.

8. It's Monday morning, and you've hit the snooze button ten times, so now you're late. After a quick shower, you run into your room to get dressed. You:

   A. Grab a soft sweater and a pair of jeans. Most of your stuff goes together, no problem.
   B. Have nothing to worry about. You plan your outfits a week in advance to make sure there are no repeats. You have a fashionable rep to protect!
   C. Put on the outfit that's neatly folded on your desk chair. You plan your outfits the night before, because you're just that organized.

SCORING:

MOSTLY A'S
You are GABRIELLA!

Sweet and feminine, your lovely style brings to mind spring meadows and sunny afternoons. You tend to choose pieces with classic touches like flowers and lace. Every now and then, you'll throw on a pair of jeans, but most of your outfits consist of cute skirts and dresses with matching tops or sweaters.

MOSTLY B'S
You are SHARPAY!

A trendy girl through and through, you like all eyes on you when you step into a room. Bold colors, slamming stripes, and of-the-minute styles are the order of the day for you. Not to mention those superfab accessories. Do you own anything that wasn't in last month's *Teen Vogue*? Doubtful.

MOSTLY C'S:
You are TAYLOR!

Your style is clean, fresh, and preppy. You want people to notice you and your smarts, not your clothes. Of course, you also want your outfits to represent your sparkling personality. That means chic blazers and skirts in power colors like red, orange, or purple. When you walk through the door, people sit up and take notice of that confident no-nonsense girl.

ARE YOU A DIVA?

Sharpay Evans is so used to being a star, she acts like one—all the time! Whether she's strutting down the hallway at school, ordering people around at her country club, or simply hanging with her brother Ryan, Sharpay makes sure that she's always the center of attention and that she gets exactly what she wants. Of course, her behavior is a bit self-centered and borderline rude. Are you in danger of being a full-time diva, too? Take our diva test and see!

1. How much time do you spend in front of a mirror (or any combination of mirrors) each day?
A. Five minutes
B. Fifteen minutes or less
C. At least an hour, maybe more

2. **Finish this sentence: "I wear rhinestones or sequins _____"**

    A. Every day.

    B. To parties.

    C. Never.

3. **True or false: You own your own microphone.**

    True

    False

4. **True or false: You keep a backup outfit in your locker in case something gets stained during the day.**

    True

    False

5. **You show up on the first day of musical rehearsals to find that you're sharing a dressing room with two other girls. You:**

    A. Accept it, but make sure you claim the side of the room with the good light and the big closet.

    B. Scream so loud you break all the mirrors.

    C. Just deal. It is what it is.

6. **The cast list is posted for the spring play. Once you've pushed your way to the front of the crowd, you find out you didn't get the lead role, but a bit part. You:**

    A. Are disappointed, but shrug it off. The girl they chose will be great, and there's always next year.

    B. Freak out and tell everyone within earshot how unfair this is.

    C. Go to the faculty adviser and offer to understudy the lead—then secretly hope the lead actress gets strep throat.

7. **You walk into school wearing your brand-new outfit and feeling gorgeous. The dress is supposed to be one-of-a-kind, but you're in the hallway for five seconds when you see some other girl wearing the same dress! You:**

   A. Storm right up to her and demand that she change her clothes. This is *your* dress!

   B. Call your mother in a panic and ask her to bring you something else to wear.

   C. Put on a sweater to set yourself apart.

8. **At summer camp, you hear that the talent-show director is putting together the order of acts for the annual show. You:**

   A. Look forward to seeing what he comes up with.

   B. Find him and demand to be put in the finale. You are, after all, the best singer at camp.

   C. Drop a hint that you'd work really hard to bring down the house—then give him a cupcake from your latest care package the next time you see him.

SCORING:

If you scored:

0-5
Diva-Free

Generally unselfish, you are not one to display superstar behavior. You try not to make a big stink when things don't go your way and definitely don't think you deserve to be in the spotlight at all times. Congrats on being so levelheaded and in control.

6-11
Minor Diva

You take things in stride, for the most part, but sometimes things seem so unfair you just have to let the world know. You know you deserve at least *some* accolades and attention for your talents, and you'd rather not have to remind people of that. But you will if you have to.

12-16
Diva Disaster

Is there ever a moment when you're *not* demanding attention? We're thinking not. Yes, we all know how fabulous you are, but if you're not careful, we're going to stop caring. Tone it down!

ARE YOU AN OVERACHIEVER?

In *High School Musical*, Gabriella and Troy try to have it all. School, clubs, sports, the musical, friends. There's nothing wrong with having lots of interests—they're what make you who you are—but it's no good if all your commitments stress you out. Everyone needs a little time to chill. Are you too busy for your own good? Take this quiz and find out.

1. **After school you can most often be found:**
    A. Chatting on the phone or watching TV.
    B. Depends on the day. Monday it's science club, Tuesday
       it's track practice, Wednesday it's yearbook . . .
    C. Probably doing homework or working out with the team.

2. **Finish this sentence: "On my last report card, I did ____"**
    A. Okay. I was proud of myself.
    B. Perfectly. All A's, of course.
    C. I don't know. I trashed it without looking at it.

3. **There's a huge history test coming up. Everyone's stressed out about it. The night before the test, you can be found:**
    A. At the library in a private kiosk, surrounded by books.
    B. Playing video games.
    C. Studying with friends.

4. Your friend is starting a new film club and needs members. She begs you to join. You've always been interested in movies, but you're already booked solid every day after school. You:

    A. Shuffle your schedule so you can fit it in and still keep all your other clubs and commitments.

    B. Tell her you're sorry, but you want to make sure you have enough time to watch TV after school.

    C. Tell her no thanks. You have the perfect number of activities right now, and one more would be too much.

5. The last time you hung out with your friends was:

    A. Friends? Who has time for friends when there are all those great fashion magazines?!

    B. Last night. We had study group followed by slices at the pizza place.

    C. *Hmm*. I'd have to check my schedule—too many things to keep track of.

6. Finish this sentence: "My personal planner is _____"

    A. Neat and clean with a few things scheduled on each weekly page.

    B. Like a battle plan. Ten things written on each day with arrows, cross outs, and all kinds of ink colors.

    C. What's a personal planner?

SCORING:

1. A-0 B-2 C-1
2. A-1 B-2 C-0
3. A-2 B-0 C-1
4. A-2 B-0 C-1
5. A-0 B-1 C-2
6. A-1 B-2 C-0

If you scored:

0-4
So Not a Joiner

When it comes to after-school activity, you're pretty much a couch potato. Clubs and teams seem like just one more "have to." And studying? Well, you only do that when pressed. We're all for relaxation, but being lazy is another story. You'd better find something that interests you, or you're not only in trouble when it comes to college apps, but you're going to be a pretty boring person, too.

5-8
Perfectly Balanced

You take school seriously, but not so seriously that it stresses you out. Plus, you've got a good balance of after-school activities to keep you involved and interested, and you still know when to take time out to have fun with your friends. Keep this up, and you just might climb the ladder to success and be happy while doing it!

9–12

Multitasking Maniac!

Think back. When was the last time you got home from school or the library before dark? When was the last time a conversation with your friends didn't revolve around grades, clubs, or sports? Can't remember? Then it's time to put down the book, drop the field hockey stick, and take a breather. Getting stressed out is bad for your health. Take a second look at your activities and make sure you're involved in things you feel strongly about. If there's a club or two that you find boring, talk to your parents about dumping them. You need a little "me" time. Try to find it!

49

WILDCAT QUIZ #4

Happy summer vacation, Wildcats! You've sailed through the first three Wildcat quizzes, all made up of questions from *High School Musical*. Good job! Now it's time for *High School Musical 2*! In the next three trivia quizzes, all the questions will come right out of the second film. Hope you have your country club employee handbook ready, because we're about to test your skills. Check it out!

1. What's the name of the country club where the Wildcats work on summer vacation?

    A. Desert Ridge

    B. Ocean View

    C. Lava Springs

2. The Wildcats' boss at the country club is named:

    A. Mr. Johnson.

    B. Mr. Fulton.

    C. Mr. Bolton.

3. **What is Gabriella's job at the country club?**
    A. Lifeguard
    B. Waitress
    C. Babysitter

4. **In *High School Musical 2*, we find out that Troy played for which team, aside from basketball, during the school year?**
    A. Football
    B. Tennis
    C. Golf

5. **Whose family owns the country club?**
    A. Troy's
    B. Kelsi's
    C. Sharpay and Ryan's

6. **What type of stage production does Sharpay put on every summer at the country club?**
    A. A musical
    B. A talent show
    C. A rock concert

7. **Who does Sharpay think is East High's "primo boy"?**
    A. Troy
    B. Zeke
    C. Ryan

8. **How does Troy get his job at the country club?**
    A. He applies for it.
    B. Sharpay gets him hired.
    C. His dad recommends him.

SCORING:

Give yourself two points for each correct answer.

If you scored:

0-4
You're scrubbing the pool!

With a score like that, you get the sorriest job at the club. Don't forget your sunscreen and knee pads!

6-10
You're on wait staff!

Not too shabby. You can be a waiter or waitress—which also means you get to race on the dinner carts during break.

12-16
You're a golf pro!

Join Troy out there on the greens in the sun! You deserve a cushy job with a score as choice as yours.

HOW MUCH IS HE CRUSHING ON YOU?

There's a lot of mystery involved when it comes to high school. Such as, should you take chemistry or biology? Why in the world would anyone schedule gym during first period? And what is that Friday lunch special made of, anyway? But the biggest mystery of all is—you guessed it—boys! You never know what they're thinking—especially the boy you're crushing on. Does he like you back, or are you two just friends? We're here to help you figure it out!

1. **When you walk into school in the morning, you go straight to your locker. Your crush is:**

     A. Nowhere to be seen.

     B. Already by your side. He walked you to school.

     C. Waiting at your locker.

2. **For your last birthday, you had a huge party and invited your crush. He:**
   A. Showed up early with a thoughtful gift he made himself.
   B. Came at the designated time and gave you a pretty bracelet.
   C. Showed up late and gave you a candle he bought at the drugstore.

3. **Last week you wore your brand-new dress to school and were feeling totally fab. When you saw your crush in the hall, he:**
   A. Said you looked nice in your new dress.
   B. Didn't even notice you.
   C. Gave you a sweet smile.

4. **You starred in this year's school play. After you took your triumphant bow on opening night, your crush:**
    A. Texted you to say he was sorry he missed it, but he'd definitely catch one of the other shows.
    B. Jumped up from the front row and handed you a bouquet of flowers.
    C. Was nowhere to be found.

5. **You have a ton to carry home from school—books, your science project, your costume for the musical. You're struggling with it all in the hallway when you bump into your crush. He:**
    A. Drops his after-school plans to walk you home.
    B. Offers to bring some of it to your house after his club meeting.
    C. Wishes you luck.

6. **You go to the movies with a bunch of friends, including your crush. Everyone wants to see the new action flick, but you're pushing for the romantic comedy. Your crush:**
    A. Takes your side and gives them five good reasons to see the comedy.
    B. Offers to go see the romantic comedy with you—alone—while everyone else takes in the action movie.
    C. Shrugs and suggests you go to the romantic comedy and meet up with them later.

SCORING:

1. A-0 B-2 C-1
2. A-2 B-1 C-0
3. A-2 B-0 C-1
4. A-1 B-2 C-0
5. A-2 B-1 C-0
6. A-1 B-2 C-0

If you scored:

0-4
Just friends.

We're sure your crush is a great guy, but it might be time to think about moving on to someone new. He clearly likes you as a friend, but someone who's crushing on you would be a bit more thoughtful and attentive. We know how hard it can be to get over a crush, but start keeping an eye out for a more worthy boy—someone who sees how very amazing you are and shows it.

5-8
He's interested.

Congratulations! Your guy is definitely interested in you. He thinks about your feelings and is there for you when you need him. If he hasn't declared his crush yet, he may just need a little time to get up the guts, or a sign from you to let him know you feel the same. (Yes, guys are nervous about saying how they really feel, too!) Do something nice for him, and maybe he'll wake up and smell the love potential.

9-12

He's crushing hard!

Wow. All signs point to major crush! He puts you ahead of himself in almost every situation, dropping his own plans to help you out and sitting through movies he doesn't want to see just so he can be with you. Why you guys haven't confessed your feelings yet is beyond us. Get up the guts and tell him how you feel. We have a hunch he's going to say he feels the same way.

BIG OOPS!

When Gabriella dumped chili fries on Sharpay in the cafeteria, Sharpay threw a fit. Gabriella, meanwhile, was so upset she could barely eat. She even told Troy that she'd just "embarrassed herself into next century." The way you handle a humiliating situation can say a lot about you. How graceful are you in an icky situation? Take this quiz and find out!

1. **You trip over someone's backpack in the cafeteria, and your lunch goes flying, causing a huge crash. Everyone applauds and laughs. You:**

   A. Take a bow and laugh it off. It happens to everyone.

   B. Run for the bathroom and hide out there for at least two classes.

   C. Freak out on the owner of the backpack. It was all his fault!

2. You're running late for homeroom, and when you finally arrive, everyone's already seated. You go to your desk only to discover someone's already sitting there. You're in the wrong room! You:

    A. Tell the class you're part of a new homeroom exchange program to help students meet new people, then introduce yourself.

    B. Apologize twenty times as you back out the door.

    C. Huffily tell the teacher that they really need to make the numbers on the doors more clear.

3. In the middle of your big solo at the spring talent show, your voice cracks. You:

    A. Keep singing. It stinks, but it happens.

    B. Freeze up and run offstage.

    C. Chew out the pianist for starting you off in the wrong key—even though she didn't.

4. You're walking down the hall at school while everyone else is in class. Thinking that you're alone, you start singing to yourself. Then you come around a corner and walk right into your crush. It's obvious he heard you. You:

    A. Laugh and ask him if he liked his private concert.

    B. Duck around him, your face burning, and run.

    C. Tell him he should watch where he's going and storm away.

5. You wake up the morning of class pictures with a huge zit on your chin. You:

    A. Dab on some cover-up, go to school, and try not to think about it.

    B. Hide behind your books all day and try to turn your face to the side for the picture.

    C. Cry and tell your parents you're staying home. They'll have to reschedule your picture.

SCORING:

MOSTLY A'S
Have a Laugh

You have a great outlook on life. You don't take anything too seriously, and you know that a moment of humiliation won't last forever. In your opinion, laughter is the best medicine for any situation. Good for you!

MOSTLY B'S
Run and Hide

When something embarrassing happens to you, you tend to freeze up or run and hide, then obsess about it for hours, if not days. This is not healthy! If you need to take a little time to yourself to cool down and catch your breath, feel free, but try not to take everything so seriously. It's bad for your complexion.

MOSTLY C'S
Tantrum Girl

Your first reaction when you do something silly is to blame it on someone else—loudly. This is not only a not-so-nice way to treat the people around you, but it makes you look mean. Try to calm your temper a bit and realize that everyone messes up now and then. It's what makes us human! If you can laugh at yourself every once in a while instead of always going the tantrum route, you'll be a much calmer and happier person.

HOW'S YOUR SCHOOL SPIRIT?

East High students are all about school spirit. For example, on the day of the championship game and Scholastic Decathlon, everybody wears red and white to show their Wildcat pride. Would you make it as a Wildcat? Take our quiz to find out!

1. **There's a huge game coming up with your rivals, and today is the pep rally. What do you wear to school?**
   - A. Regular clothes
   - B. Something simple in school colors
   - C. A team sweatshirt and hat, with your face painted and a foam finger on your hand

2. **The booster club has decided to paint all the lockers in school colors to pump up school spirit. They're looking for volunteers to help with the big project. You:**
   - A. Are the first to sign up and stay until dark to help.
   - B. Think it's a lame idea and put stickers on your locker to make it harder to paint.
   - C. Think it could be fun for an afternoon and offer to paint one or two lockers.

WILDCATS

3. It's the night of the big basketball game. You can be found:
- A. On the sidelines, dressed as the team mascot.
- B. In the stands.
- C. On your couch at home.

4. How many school functions have you attended this month? (Include club meetings, dances, practices, and games.)
- A. 0
- B. 1—4
- C. 5+

5. Last year your class sold chocolate bars to raise money for the class trip. What became of your box of chocolate?
- A. You sold all the chocolate bars to neighbors and friends in the first two days, then asked the class adviser for another box to sell.
- B. You ate them all.
- C. You sold them to your parents.

6. You just heard the school board is talking about shutting down one of your school's teams. You:
- A. Could not care less.
- B. Sign a petition to stop it.
- C. Organize a student protest at the next board meeting.

Did You Know?

Before *High School Musical*:

- Olesya Rulin (Kelsi) trained as a classical ballerina and worked as a model.
- Monique Coleman (Taylor) worked as a babysitter and was president of a girls' club in high school.
- Vanessa Hudgens (Gabriella) was homeschooled since seventh grade, so she never actually went to a high school!

SCORING:

1. A-0 B-1 C-2
2. A-2 B-0 C-1
3. A-2 B-1 C-0
4. A-0 B-1 C-2
5. A-2 B-0 C-1
6. A-0 B-1 C-2

If you scored:

0-4
Pride Schmide

When it comes to school spirit, you have no interest. You frown upon people who wear the school colors on game day and think pep rallies are nothing but a good way to get out of class. Maybe you should try getting into the swing of things—at least a bit. We're not talking about changing your style or suddenly carrying pom-poms everywhere, but try opening your mouth and cheering at the next rally or volunteering to work the snack bar at the next game. Being involved can be fun, make you feel good about yourself and your school, and can introduce you to new people. There's no downside to that!

5-8

School Spirit Is Cool—Sometimes

You've got pride, in moderation. You're not one to go bonkers in the stands or paint your face on game day, but you'll be there to cheer on your teams when it counts. Plus you support your class and your clubs with hard work and a good attitude. You're definitely an asset to your school.

9-12

True to Your School!

You wear school colors practically every day. Not only do you volunteer to help with spirit projects, but you join every team and club you can manage. You're always trying to come up with ways to promote school spirit and have never missed a game or pep rally. We foresee a picture of you in the yearbook, wearing face paint and a football jersey. The caption underneath reads: "Most School Spirit."

ARE YOU DETENTION MATERIAL?

Ever wondered just how fast Darbus would stick you in detention? Well, it all depends on how big of a rule-breaker you are. And whether or not you'd dare to whip out your cell phone in her presence, of course. Are you an immediate detention-getter like Chad, or are you a goody-goody like Jason? Take our quiz, and see if you'll be spending your afternoon building sets with the gang.

1. **Have you ever interrupted a teacher while he or she was in the middle of a sentence?**
   A. Absolutely. I do that every day.
   B. Never. Not without raising my hand.
   C. Once or twice, if it was really important.

2. **Ms. Darbus is at the front of the room, rambling on about the time she starred in *Twelfth Night*. You:**
   A. Are loving every minute of the story and can't tear your attention away. In fact, you ask a few questions to show your interest.
   B. Are doing a comical interpretation of Ms. Darbus for your friends in the back of the room.
   C. Are staring out the window, dreaming of summer.

3. **You walk into homeroom five seconds after the final bell rings. Ms. Darbus points out that you're late. You say:**
   A. "I'm so sorry, but Principal Matsui wanted to talk to me about leading a new volunteer program."
   B. "I'm so sorry. It won't happen again."
   C. "Whatever."

4. You've been sitting in homeroom for one minute, and Ms. Darbus has already handed out five detentions to your friends. She's clearly on a roll. You:

    A. Keep your mouth shut so she'll have no reason to make you her next victim.

    B. Smirk. You can't help it. Everyone looks so miserable, it's funny.

    C. Ask Ms. Darbus if she woke up on the wrong side of the bed. Then count the seconds until she gives *you* detention.

5. Ms. Darbus gives your best friend detention—the friend you were supposed to go shopping with after school. You:

    A. Tell Ms. Darbus she can't do that to you.

    B. Roll your eyes and grumble under your breath about how unfair it is.

    C. Open your planner to figure out when you and your friend can reschedule.

6. How many times have you been caught talking on your cell phone during school hours?

    A. Never

    B. Once or twice

    C. At least once a week, every week since I got the thing

SCORING:

1. A-0 B-2 C-1   4. A-2 B-1 C-0
2. A-2 B-0 C-1   5. A-0 B-1 C-2
3. A-2 B-1 C-0   6. A-2 B-1 C-0

If you scored:

0-4
"Mom? I'm gonna be home late."

You are a Darbus nightmare! You always forget to turn off your cell phone, can't keep your mouth shut, and don't pay attention when she's talking about her favorite thing in the world—the theater! Better get your act in gear, or you'll be painting and hammering every day after school.

5-8
"Slipups happen now and then."

Ms. Darbus generally likes you—you respect most of her rules most of the time—but every once in a while you trip up. You just have to take the cell phone call or can't seem to get to class on time. The good news? At the next musical performance, you'll be able to lean in and whisper to the person next to you, "See that tree? I painted that."

9–12

"Detention? What's detention?"

You are Ms. Darbus's favorite student! Or not. Since you never get detention, you're no help to her and her set crew. Still, with a homeroom full of cutups and cell-phone abusers, you're a refreshing change!

WILDCAT QUIZ #5

You just keep coming back for more, don't you? Troy and the rest of the Wildcats would be impressed with your never-say-die attitude. Ready to show your skills on another *High School Musical 2* quiz? Well, lucky for you, we're ready to give you one! Enjoy!

1. **What's the title of the award that is given away at the end of the talent show?**
    A. The Superstar Award
    B. The Emmy® Award
    C. The Star Dazzle Award

2. **Who falls into the pool at the country club and gets "saved" by Gabriella?**
    A. Troy
    B. Sharpay
    C. Ryan

3. What is Chad planning to buy with the money he earns at Lava Springs over the summer?

   A. A car

   B. A boat

   C. A basketball hoop

4. Troy and Gabriella attempt to have a picnic out on the golf course at Lava Springs. It's cut short by:

   A. The sprinklers coming on.

   B. An army of ants.

   C. Chad and Zeke wanting to play ball.

5. In *High School Musical 2*, Kelsi writes a duet for:

   A. Ryan and Sharpay

   B. Gabriella and Troy

   C. Chad and Taylor

6. In order to spend more time with Troy, Sharpay fakes being bad at what sport?

   A. Basketball

   B. Frisbee

   C. Golf

7. What does Mr. Fulton do to Troy when he catches Troy and Gabriella swimming after the pool has closed?

   A. Fires him

   B. Promotes him to assistant golf pro

   C. Gives him a noogie

8. According to Sharpay's club friends, what color is just "*so* this year"?

   A. Green

   B. Purple

   C. Red

72

SCORING:

Give yourself two points
for each correct answer.

If you scored:

0–4
Opening Act

Come on, Wildcat!
With a score
like that, you're
stinking up the
stage!

6–10
Minor Star

You've got a few
moves and can hit
some sick notes.
But you've got
a bit more work
to do before you
land the finale.

12–16
**Star Dazzle
Award**

You're a
superstar—and
deserve to win
best act in the
Midsummer's
Night Star Dazzle
Talent Show!

ARE YOU SOCIAL OR SHY?

What if *High School Musical* had never happened? It might not have, if Gabriella hadn't been dragged up onto the karaoke stage against her will. Gabriella would have much rather sat on the sidelines with her book then get up there and sing in the spotlight. But if she hadn't, she never would have met Troy. Some of us are shy by nature, while others are social butterflies, ready and willing to meet new people and try new things. How are you in a party situation? Take our quiz and find out!

1. **The entire school is talking about this huge party the new guy at school is throwing this weekend. When you hear about it your first thought is:**
   A. I hope I don't get invited.
   B. I can't wait!
   C. I hope someone I know will be there.

2. **A girl from your homeroom invites you to her Sweet 16 sleepover party. You:**
   A. Immediately accept the invitation. You love a good sleepover and gossip fest.
   B. Wait to see if any of your friends are invited. You need a built-in group to talk to.
   C. Decline. You can't imagine what you would talk about.

3. At camp orientation, your counselor announces that you're going to play a get-to-know-you game. It involves you walking up to other people in the cabin and asking them questions about themselves. You:

A. Hide in the corner and hope she forgets to include you.

B. Grin and bear it, and let other people come to you.

C. Are the first person to talk to every single person in your bunk.

4. Your parents tell you that you have to join a new club at school, both to meet new people and to flesh out your college applications. You choose:

   A. Foreign Language Club. It's small, doesn't meet very often, and you already know and like most of the people in it.
   B. Booster Club. They get involved with all the teams and events and are always chatting people up at games and pep rallies.
   C. Computer Club. You hear all you have to do is sit at a computer for an hour after school and work on projects. Almost zero interaction with others.

5. You and your friends decide to go to the Holiday Dance in one big group. At the dance, you can be found:

   A. Dancing in the center of the floor with all your girls—plus some other people you just met.
   B. Standing near the wall watching the clock.
   C. Chatting with your BFF near the punch bowl.

6. The single most important thing to bring with you when attending a party is:

   A. A good friend so you know you'll have someone to talk to.
   B. Just yourself—you can get the party started without any help!
   C. A cell phone so you can call your mom and leave early.

SCORING:

1.	A-0	B-2	C-1	4.	A-1	B-2	C-0
2.	A-2	B-1	C-0	5.	A-2	B-0	C-1
3.	A-0	B-1	C-2	6.	A-1	B-2	C-0

If you scored:

0-4

Quiet as a Mouse

You, a party animal? No way! You would much rather be sitting in a corner, reading or watching TV, then meeting people and laughing it up. But meeting new people can be fun. So the next time you're at a party feeling timid, try to make yourself talk to at least two or three people. It might be hard, but it can also be rewarding. Remember what stepping out of her shell did for Gabriella—she met Troy! Now that's a reward that's worth the effort!

5-8

Semisocial

Sometimes shy, sometimes outgoing, you have to assess a party situation before you know which mood you'll be in. You're best in a group of close friends, but with them by your side to boost you up, you're also able to meet new people and stretch your limits. Don't worry if you're not always in the mood to chat all night long, though. Every once in a while it's cool to, well, play it cool.

9-12

Social Butterfly

The girl in the center of the dance floor? That's you. The girl keeping everyone else at the slumber party up all night long gabbing? That's you, too. And the girl who knows every single person at school? Also you! You know how to have fun, keep the conversation flowing, and make the people around you laugh. Even better, you enjoy it. You are a true people person.

IS YOUR HEAD IN THE GAME?

Being a true Wildcat is all about teamwork. Troy may have hit the winning shot in the championship game, but even he admits he couldn't have done it without a few perfect passes from his teammates. Troy definitely knows there's no "I" in "team." But could you be as humble as he is after such a fabulous performance? Are you a team player or a superstar? Take our quiz and find out!

1. **Your school requires that you participate in a varsity sport in order to get credit for gym class. You choose:**
   - A. Soccer, lacrosse, basketball, or some other team sport.
   - B. Cross-country running or long-distance swimming.
   - C. Doubles tennis.

2. **It's down to the final seconds in your hockey game. You're speeding down the ice with the puck, dodging all defenders. The goalie's sights are set on you, but your teammate is open on the goalie's blind side. You:**

   A. Pass your teammate the puck so he/she can make the shot.

   B. Take the shot. This goalie so does not have your number.

   C. Quickly assess the situation. If the goalie is blocking your angle to the net, you pass to your teammate. If you see an opening, you try to make the shot.

3. **You've just won the MVP award for your stellar basketball season. The first people you thank in your speech are:**

   A. Your mother and father for giving you such athletic genes.

   B. Your teammates for supporting you all season.

   C. Your coach for teaching you the value of teamwork and helping you improve your own skills on the court.

4. **During gym class, two captains are choosing teams for a soccer game. You:**

   A. Are confident you'll be chosen first. Everyone knows you're the best player in the class.

   B. Keep your fingers crossed that other good players will be chosen for your team—you want your team to win after all.

   C. Chill out about who gets chosen—no matter who's on your team, you know if you work together that you'll have fun playing.

81

5. You and your friends all signed up for softball, but your coach keeps sticking you in the outfield, which bores you. You:

    A. Stick it out until the end of the season. You made a commitment, and your team needs you.

    B. Quit. You don't like wasting your time. Your friends will understand.

    C. Ask the coach if you can try playing other positions.

6. Your cheerleading squad is going to vote for a captain at practice this Friday. You spend the week:

    A. Watching your teammates to see who would make a good leader.

    B. Acting the part of a good leader so that you'll be elected.

    C. Campaign hard, baking cookies and giving your teammates presents.

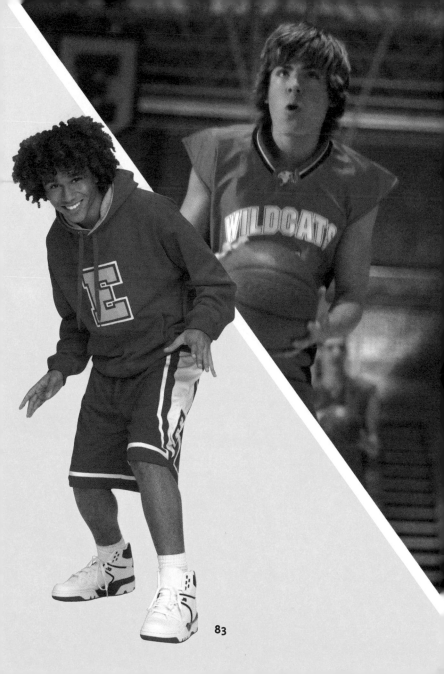

SCORING:

1. A-2   B-0   C-1
2. A-2   B-0   C-1
3. A-0   B-2   C-1
4. A-0   B-1   C-2
5. A-2   B-0   C-1
6. A-2   B-1   C-0

If you scored:

0–4

Every team has a star, and that star is you.

One question: How do you walk upright with an ego that size weighing you down? So you're good at your sport. That's fantastic. But you'd better stop reminding everyone of that every chance you get and start supporting your teammates, or no one's going to want to play with you.

5–8

There's no "I" in "team," but there is one in "win."

You know how to share the glory some of the time, but there are moments when you feel you're the only one who can help your team win. It's good to shine on the court or the field, but try not to forget there are other players out there, too. You're not only there to support them, but they are there to support you! Let them help out every once in a while, and you might just have more fun.

9–12

Total Team Player

You know that every win is a team effort, no matter who scores the winning shot, and you make sure your teammates know that, too. Yours is a team we want to be on!

ARE YOU CLIQUISH OR COOL?

In the beginning of *High School Musical*, it's pretty clear that Taylor isn't so fond of the athletes and cheerleaders. She picks on the jocks in the hallway and even jokes that the cheerleaders have their own language. There's no way she'd ever want to hang out with any of the people in those cliques. Of course, she later learns that none of them is exactly what they seem, but it takes a while for her to get there. Do you judge the people in other cliques too harshly, or do you think anyone and everyone has the potential to be cool? Take our quiz to find out just how clique-obsessed you really are.

1. **The new girl at school sits down with you and your friends at your usual table in the cafeteria. She dresses differently than you guys do and doesn't seem to fit in. You:**
    A. Introduce yourself and make her feel welcome.
    B. Ask where she's from and pepper her with questions to find out what she likes and dislikes.
    C. Ask her what she thinks she's doing. Your table is full, thanks.

2. **When was the last time you hung out with someone outside your own clique?**
    A. Every day
    B. At my last club meeting
    C. Never

3. **You had a best friend in grade school, but you've grown apart and are in different cliques. When you receive an invite to her Sweet 16 party, you:**
    A. Definitely go. You may not talk much anymore, but you were once good friends, and if she wants you there, you're in.
    B. Make an appearance, but not for too long. You don't want those people to start thinking you're going to be hanging out with them all the time.
    C. Laugh over the invitation with your friends. What, is she kidding? Like you'd ever hang out with those kids.

4. **For your birthday, your mom gives you a new black jacket which you adore. You wear it to school, and your preppy friends pick on you for looking like a goth. You:**
    - A. Say, "Whatever. I like it." And keep wearing it.
    - B. Tell them your mom bought it for you and made you wear it.
    - C. Take it off and shove it in the bottom of your locker with your old gym socks.

5. **You're really interested in photography and want to join the photo club. But none of your friends are in it, and it's almost exclusively made up of this one other clique—a bunch of people you've never talked to. You:**
    - A. Join the club and do your best to make friends there. After all, they share at least one of your interests.
    - B. Join the club, but keep to yourself. You don't really need to know these people.
    - C. Don't join. If you do, everyone will think you're one of *them*.

6. **You're at the mall with your mom when you bump into a girl from a different clique, and she's with *her* mom. Your mothers start chatting happily. Apparently they know each other from the PTA. You:**
    - A. Talk to the girl. You may not know her well, but you've seen her around. Plus it would be awkward if you didn't talk to her.
    - B. Say hello, then pray for your mother to clam up so you can go.
    - C. Totally ignore her. If anyone saw you talking to her, it would be the end of your social life.

SCORING:

MOSTLY A'S
Friends with Everyone!

You are an open-minded person who knows that looks are not everything. You never judge a book by its cover or a person by her clique. We have a feeling your life is a lot more interesting because of it! Kudos!

MOSTLY B'S
Somewhat Sociable

Let's say your mind is not totally open, but not closed either. Your mind is ajar. You let in some outsiders, but are judgmental of others. Ever take a look at your reasons for picking and choosing the people you'll talk to? Maybe you should. If you still think your reasoning is, well, reasonable, then fine. But maybe you'll decide to try opening the door a bit wider.

MOSTLY C'S
Stick to Your Clique!

You, my friend, are completely shut off. Wait, can I even call you my friend? It seems like the list of people who are allowed to do that is a very short one. Maybe you think you know what you like, and that's a good thing. But unless you try new things—which includes getting to know some new people—you might miss out on some pretty cool experiences.

WILDCAT QUIZ #6

Congratulations! You've done it, Wildcat! You've made it to the very last trivia quiz. Think you know all there is to know about *High School Musical 2*? Well, we've got some stumpers for you, so get ready for a challenge. Without further ado, welcome to your final exam!

1. **What's the name of the mascot of the University of Albuquerque, where Troy is thinking about going to college?**
   A. The Wildcats
   B. The Cowboys
   C. The Redhawks

2. **After caddying for Sharpay and her family, Chad cools off his tired feet in what?**
   A. A bucket of ice
   B. The pool
   C. A vat of ice cream

3. When Troy misses a date with Gabriella, Taylor claims he has what?
    A. Chicken pox
    B. Boy disease
    C. Amnesia

4. When the Wildcats organize a pickup game after work, what sport do they play?
    A. Football
    B. Lacrosse
    C. Softball

5. Who directs the Wildcats in their dance number for the Midsummer's Night Star Dazzle Talent Show?
    A. Ryan
    B. Mr. Fulton
    C. Coach Bolton

6. What does Sharpay do backstage when she gets nervous?
    A. Screams
    B. Cries
    C. Eats

7. Who eventually goes home with the Star Dazzle Award?
    A. Sharpay
    B. Gabriella
    C. Ryan

8. Who surprises all the Wildcats by offering to help clean up the club after the talent show?
    A. Mr. Fulton
    B. Sharpay
    C. Ms. Darbus

ANSWERS:

1. C   5. A
2. A   6. C
3. B   7. C
4. C   8. B

SCORING:

Give yourself two points for each correct answer.

If you scored:

0–4
Back to Work!

With a score like that, you don't deserve a break. Better get back in the country club kitchen and scrub those dishes.

6–10
Take Your Fifteen

Take a break and play some ball with your friends. You've earned some time out in the sun.

12–16
Summer of Fun

That's a fabulous score! You've done your work well, Wildcat. Now, go have some fun!